D1552684

BOB DYLAN

Copyright © 2005 by Essential Works Ltd. All rights reserved.
Printed in China. No part of this book may be used or reproduced
in any manner whatsoever without written permission except in
the case of reprints in the context of reviews. For information,
write Andrews McMeel Publishing, an Andrews McMeel Universal
company, 4520 Main Street, Kansas City, Missouri 64111.

Library of Congress Cataloging-in-Publication-Data

Bob Dylan: inspirations.
   p. cm.
  ISBN 0-7407-5455-6
  1. Dylan, Bob 1941---Quotations. 1. Title.

PS3554.Y56A6 2005
782.42164'092--dc22

ISBN-13: 978-0-7407-5455-5
ISBN-10: 0-7407-5455-6
Library of Congress Control Number: 2005048013

05 06 07 08 09 IMA 10 9 8 7 6 5 4 3 2 1

Produced by Essential Works
168a Camden Street, London, NW1 9PT, England

Designed by Grant Scott

The publishers have made every reasonable effort to contact all
copyright holders. Any errors that may have occurred are
inadvertent and anyone who has not been contacted is invited to
write to the publishers so that a full acknowledgment may be
made in subsequent editions of this work.

Attention: Schools and Businesses
Andrews McMeel books are available at quantity discounts with
bulk purchase for educational, business, or sales promotional use.
For information, please write to: Special Sales Department,
Andrews McMeel Publishing, 4520 Main Street, Kansas City,
Missouri 64111.

Bob Dylan photographs
courtesy of Topfoto.co.uk;
circus tent photograph
courtesy of Flatgaroo
Production AB/Gustav
Kaiser; 1965 Triumph
Bonneville photograph
courtesy of Paul T. Legris;
planet, storm, clouds, and
refinery photographs
courtesy of Photodisc Inc.

Printed in China

inspirations

BOB DYLAN

**Andrews McMeel
Publishing**

Kansas City

WO

I AM MY

RDS

There was a violent, angry emotion running through me back then. I just played the guitar and harmonica and sang those songs and that was it.

The whole
counterculture
was one
big scarecrow
wearing
dead leaves.
It had
no purpose
in my life.

I stood on the highway during a blizzard snowstorm believing in the mercy of the world and headed east, didn't have nothing

but my guitar
and suitcase.
That was
my whole world.

I knew that I had to get to New York.
I'd been dreaming about that for a long time.

Writing a song is what I can do and know how to do and need to do.

I don't call myself a poet because

I don't like the word.

I'm a trapeze   artist.

I always knew that there was something out there

that I needed to get to.

A

HE

RO

s someone who understands the responsibility that comes with his

FREEDOM

Truth is chaos.

Maybe beauty is chaos.

The point is not understanding what I write but

feeling it.

Time goes by very fast

up there onstage. I think of what not to do rather than what to do.

I'm just as good a singer as Caruso . . . a good singer, have to listen closely, but I hit all those notes and I can hold my breath

3 times as long if I want to.

The back wheel locked up,
        I think. I lost control,
swerving from left to right.
        Next thing I know I was
someplace I'd never heard
        of—Middletown, I think—
with my face cut up, so I got
        some scars and my neck
busted up pretty good.
        I saw my whole life pass
in front of me.

**If I wasn't Bob Dylan,
I'd probably think that Bob Dylan
has a lot of answers myself.**

ALL THE TRUTH IN THE WORLD ADDS UP TO ONE BIG

I had some amazing projections when I was a kid, but not since then. And those visions have been strong enough to keep me going through to today.

I had some amazing projections when I was a kid, but not since then. And those visions have been strong enough to keep me going through to today.

The first song I wrote was a song

to Brigitte Bardot.

Who cares about tomorrow and yesterday?

People don't live there, they live NOW.

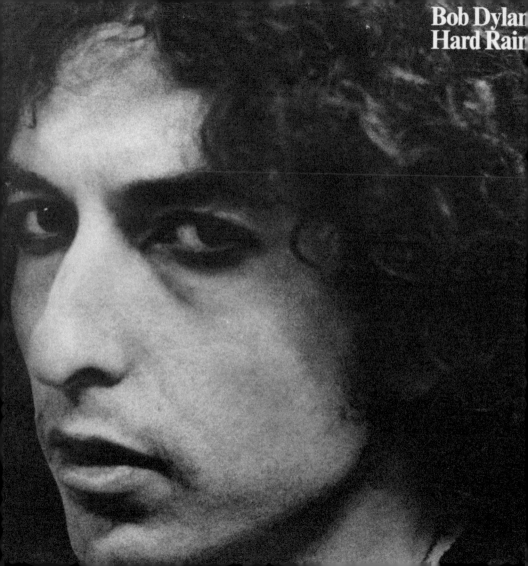

Bob Dylan
Hard Rain

Just because you like my stuff doesn't mean I owe you anything.

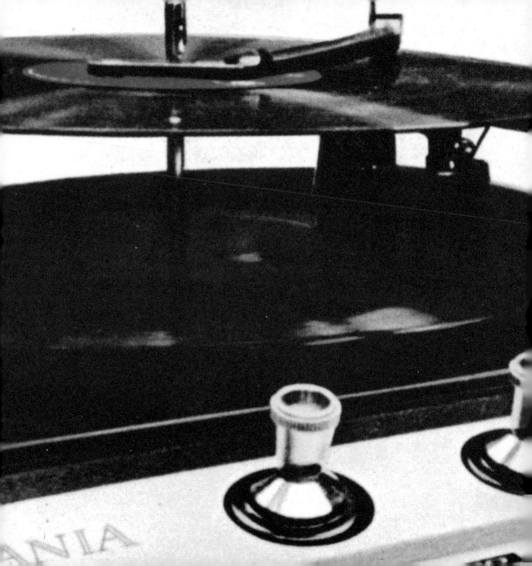

I think of myself as a song and dance man.

The closest I ever got to the sound I hear in my mind was . . . that thin, that wild mercury sound. It's metallic and bright gold.

I don't know
how much I make.
Sometimes I ask,
sometimes I don't.
I don't know
what I spend it on,
it just falls through holes
in my pocket.

I believe in Hank Williams singing
"I Saw the Light."

I've seen the light, too.

Cameras make ghosts out of people.

Be.
Be p.

eriod.
is

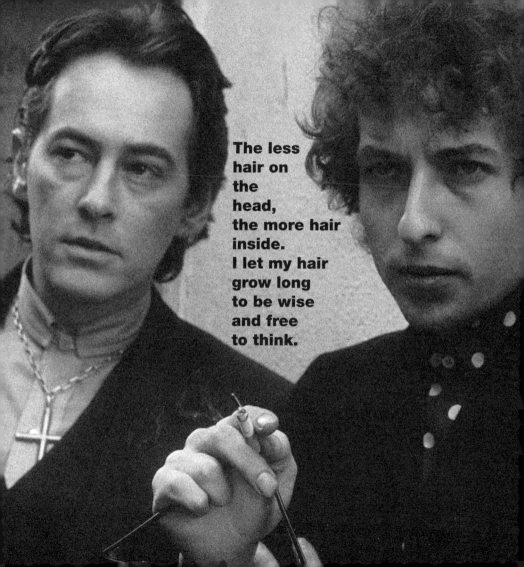

The less
hair on
the
head,
the more hair
inside.
I let my hair
grow long
to be wise
and free
to think.

I LOOK AT PEOPLE AS IDEAS.

I DON'T LOOK AT THEM AS PEOPLE.

JOHN BROWN

Bob Dylan) sung by Blind Boy Gru

ohn Brown was sabered down while fighting for th

3,000,000 enslaved Americans. His reward was a

This modern day John Brown fights like hell fo:

except maybe to give his neurotic mother somethi

eighbors about. He trades various of his

a set of nice, shiny medals. With these medals

er can get a ride anytime on a New York subway t

If you examine the songs, I don't believe you're going to find anything in there that says that I'm a spokesman for anybody or anything, really.

They were songs . . . they weren't sermons.

Muse

ums
are cemeteries

They can't hurt me. Sure, they can crush you
and kill you. They can lay you out on 42nd
and Broadway and put hoses on you
and flush you in the sewers and put you
on the subway and carry you out to Coney Island
and bury you on the Ferris wheel.
But I refuse to sit here and worry about dying.

I don't like
the Democratic-
Republican system.
I like monarchies, kings, and queens.

When I get involved in something, I get totally involved. I don't just play around on the fringes.

I went over my whole life.
I went over my whole childhood.
I didn't talk to anyone for a week
after Elvis died.
If it wasn't for Elvis
and Hank Williams,
I couldn't be doing what I do today.

BOB DYLAN HIGHWAY 61 REVISITED

We all like motorcycles to some degree.

You fail

only when you let death creep in and take over a part of your life that should be alive.

I've conceded the fact
that there is
no understanding of anything.
At best, just winks of the eye
and that is all
I'm looking for now, I guess.

The times cry for the truth . . .
and people want to hear the truth
and that's just what they're hearing
in good folk music today.

BROADSIDE

© Produced with the cooperation of
FOLKWAYS RECORDS, N.Y. USA
1964 by Folkways Records, N.Y. USA

SIDE II

Band 1: FAUBUS' FOLLIES (P. La Farge) Peter La Farge
Band 2: I WILL NOT GO UNDER THE GROUND (B. Dylan)
    Happy Traum
Band 3: ONLY A HOBO (B. Dylan) - TALKIN' DEVIL (B. Dylan)
    Blind Boy Grunt
Band 4: AIN'T GONNA LET SEGREGATION TURN US AROUND
    Freedom Singers
Band 5: GO LIMP (A. Comfort) Matt McGinn
Band 6: BIZNESS AIN'T DEAD (W. Guthrie)
    New World Singers
Band 7: THE CIVIL DEFENSE SIGN (M. Spoelstra)
    Mark Spoelstra
Band 8: I CAN SEE A NEW DAY (L. Rice)
    New World Singers

B-301 B

Ain't nobody can say anything honest in the United States. Every place you look is cluttered with phoneys and lies.

I was never going to be
anything else, never.
I was playing when
I was twelve years old
and all I wanted to do was
play my guitar.

The town didn't have a rabbi and it was time for me to be bar mitzvahed. Suddenly a rabbi showed up under strange circumstances for only a year. He and his wife got off the bus in the middle of winter. He was an old man from Brooklyn who had a white beard and wore a black hat and black clothes. They put him upstairs above a café, which was the local hangout, a rock 'n' roll café. I used to go there every day to learn this stuff either after school or after dinner.
After studying with him for an hour or so, I'd come down and boogie.

You can't eat applause for breakfast.

I can create several orbits

that travel and intersect

each other

and are set up

in a metaphysical way.

Keep a clean nose and carry a lightbulb.

**The worst times of my life were
when I tried to find something in the past.**

PEOPLE NEED TO BE ENCOURAGED, NOT STEPPED ON AND PUT IN A

STRAITJACKET

If you try to be anyone but yourself, you will fail;

if you are not true to your own heart, you will fail.

Then again, there's no success like failure.

BEING NOTICED CAN BE A BURDEN

JESUS GOT HIMSELF CRUCIFIED

NOTICED

BECAUSE HE GOT HIMSELF

So I disappear a lot.

No, I don't believe in anything.
No, why should I believe in anything?

You take it from there.

Popular songs are the only art form that describes the temper of the times; that's where people hang out. It's not in books; it's not on the stage; it's not in the galleries.

My lawyer used to tell me there
was a future in movies.
So I said, "What kind of future?"
He said, "Well, if you can come up
with a script outline and
get money from a big distributor,"
but I knew I couldn't work that
way. I can't betray my vision on a
little piece of paper in hopes
of getting money from somebody.

The highest
form of song
is prayer.

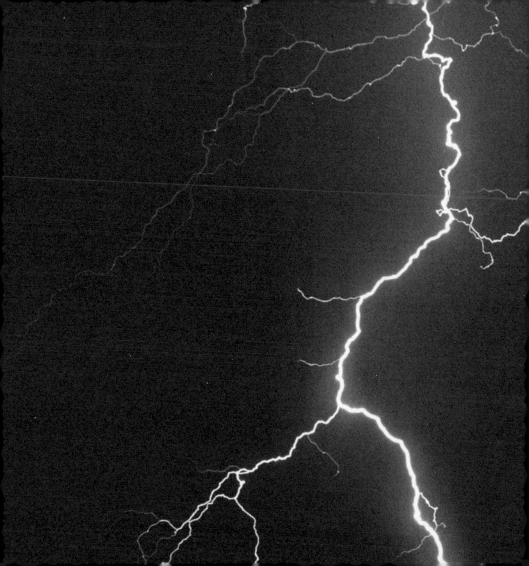

I like storms. I like to stay up during a storm.

**You call yourself what you want to call yourself.
This is the land of the**

**Drugs were never
that
big a thing with me.
I could take
them or leave them.**

Never hung me ^{up}**.**

I'm not sure people understood a lot of what I was writing about. I don't even know if I would understand them if I believed everything that has been written about them by imbeciles who wouldn't know the first thing about writing songs. I've always said the organized media propagated me as something I never pretended to be . . . all this spokesman of conscience thing. A lot of my songs were definitely misinterpreted by people who didn't know any better, and it goes on today.

I'm an easygoing kind of fellow, you know. I forgive and forget.

Don't matter how much money you got, there's only two kinds of people: there's saved people and there's lost people.

Chance
RECORDS, INC.
CHICAGO, ILL.

SIDE ONE

BD88-2-A

BOB DYLAN
SUBTERRANEAN PHILADELPHIA BLUES
SUBTERRANEAN HOMESICK BLUES
JUST LIKE A WOMAN
HIGHWAY 61
IT'S ALL OVER NOW BABY BLUE
I'LL BE YOU BABY TONIGHT
LOVE MINUS ZERO
29:40

You can't do
something forever.
I did it once,
and I can
do other things now.

My father probably thought the capital of the world was wherever he was at the time. It couldn't possibly be anyplace else. Where he and his wife were in their own home, that, for them, was the capital of the world.

J ♥

You feel like an impostor when someone thinks you're something

and you're not.

The press, the media,
they're not the judge—
God's the judge.
The only person you have to
think about lying twice to
is either yourself or to God.

The press isn't either of them.

Is that me who you saw up there?

ROYAL
ALBERT HALL
- A Recorded Concert -

AH-LP-3A
SIDE 1

33 1/3 RPM
MONO

TELL ME MAMA
I DON'T BELIEVE YOU
BABY LET ME FOLLOW YOU DOWN
JUST LIKE TOM THUMB BLUES

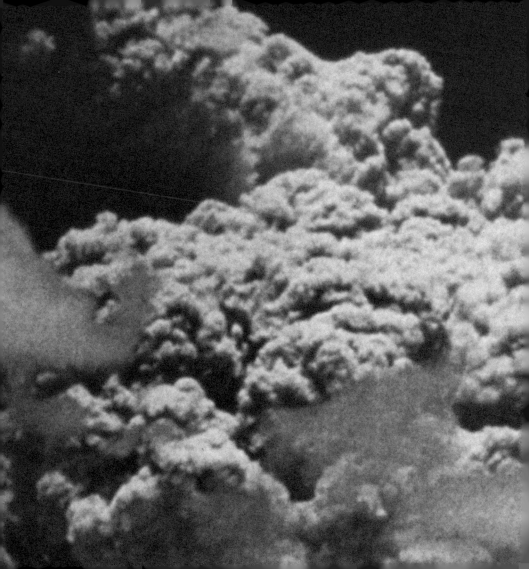

I can be jubilant one moment and pensive the next, and a cloud could go by and make that happen.

I'm inconsistent, even to myself.

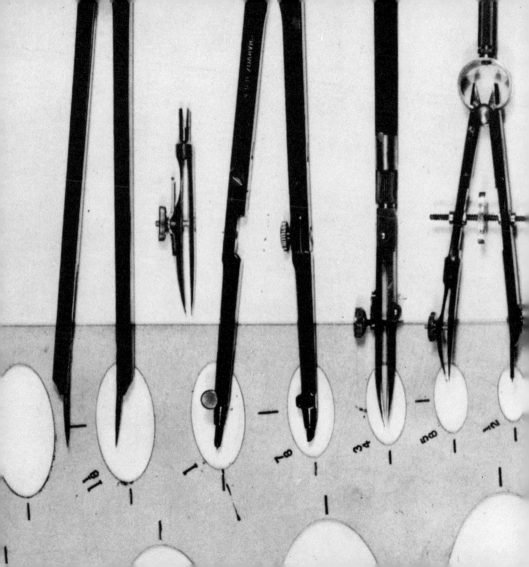

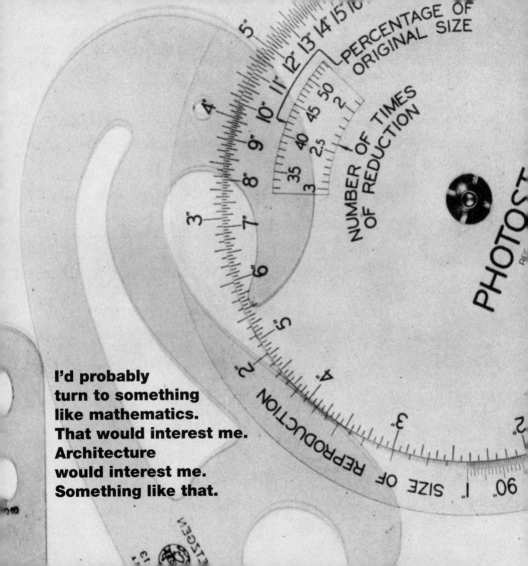

I'd probably turn to something like mathematics. That would interest me. Architecture would interest me. Something like that.

I don't think there are any new souls on Earth. Caesar, Alexander, Nebuchadnezzar, Baal, Nimrod. They've all been here time and time again. Spirit talks to flesh—flesh talks to spirit. But you never know which is which. I'm not seeking the truth—nor was I ever. I was born knowing the truth. Everybody is. Trouble is they get it knocked out of them before they can walk.

What
we
all
know
is
that
you
can't
hide
on
a
dark
street
from
the
demon
within

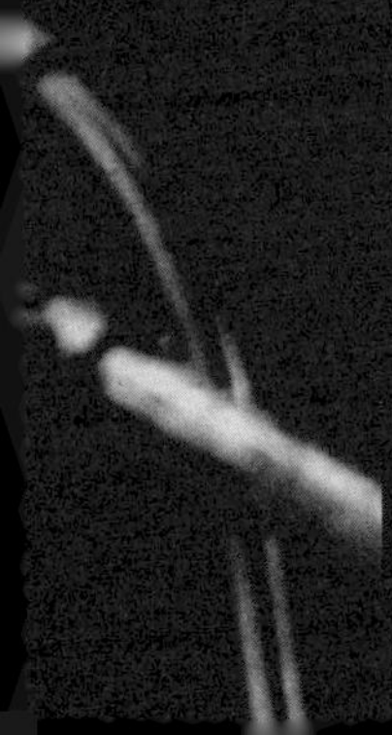

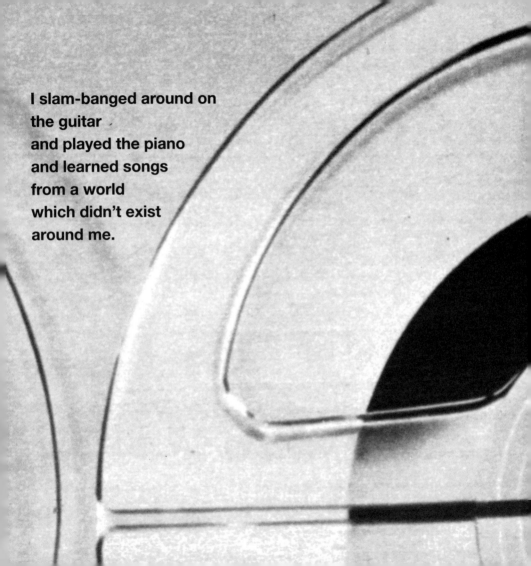

I slam-banged around on
the guitar
and played the piano
and learned songs
from a world
which didn't exist
around me.

I NEVER WANTED TO BE A PROPHET OR SAVIOR.

ELVIS

MAYBE.

When you get beyond
a certain year,
after you go on for
a certain number of
years, you realize,
hey, life is kind
of short anyway.
And you might as well
say the way you feel.

None of us are immune to the spirit of the age. It affects us whether we know it or whether we like it or not.

We have to be able to hear that voice. I'm through listening to other people tell me how to live my life . . . I'm just doing now what I feel is right for me, for my own self.

WE ALL WANT

TO STOP TIME

It was never my intention to become a big star. It happened, and there was nothing I could do about it.